# ANIMALS
## Live in Homes

by Nadia Ali

PEBBLE
a capstone imprint

Published by Pebble, an imprint of Capstone
1710 Roe Crest Drive, North Mankato, Minnesota 56003
capstonepub.com

Library of Congress Cataloging-in-Publication Data is available on the Library
of Congress website.

ISBN: 9780756571924 (hardcover)
ISBN: 9780756571870 (paperback)
ISBN: 9780756571887 (ebook PDF)

Summary: A bear sleeps in a den. A snake might coil around a branch to rest.
A crab carries its home on its back! Find out where all kinds of animals live—in
the water, up in the trees, or burrowed underground.

Editorial Credits:
Editor: Kristen Mohn; Designer: Tracy Davies; Media Researcher: Svetlana
Zhurkin; Production Specialist: Katy LaVigne

Image Credits:
Dreamstime: Carol R. Montoya, 6, Kuritafsheen, 15; Getty Images: DejaVu
Designs, 17, EyeEm/Ralf Lehmann, 29, geoffsp, 22, Irina Kulikova, 28,
jamesvancouver, 26, Juan Carlos Vindas, 12, slowmotiongli, 20; Shutterstock
Arh-sib, 1, 10, artcasta, 5, belizar, 25, brian hewitt, 4, Gerry Bishop, 18, Kerrie
W, 24, Miroslav Halama, 14, Nick Biemans, 21, Petra Todtova, cover, pictoplay,
23, Pix Box, 27, Powerofflowers, 8, Rejean Bedard, 7, 9, 19, Sergey Uryadnikov,
11, slowmotiongli, 13, Steve Byland, 16

All internet sites appearing in back matter were available and accurate when
this book was sent to press.

# TABLE OF CONTENTS

Words in **bold** are in the glossary.

# What Homes Do Animals Live In?

Animals live in different homes, just like you! Some of their homes are hidden below ground. Some are high up in the trees. Some animals carry their home on their back!

Let's find out where animals live.

# Dens

Black bears live in the forest. They find a cave or hollow for a den. They make a cozy bed of leaves. Then bears take a long nap from winter to spring. Zzzzz . . .

Beavers live near rivers. They build a bank den close to the water. It is made of grass, branches, and mud. Inside is a dry area called a lodge. The lodge keeps the family and its food safe.

*Splish, splash!* River otters build dens near rivers, lakes, or ponds. The opening to the den may be underwater! Some otters find dens that beavers or muskrats have left. Otters move in and make their home.

A fox finds or digs a den in the forest. The den keeps fox babies safe from **predators**. After the babies grow up, foxes use dens to stay warm or to store food.

A squirrel scurries to a hole in a tree. This is its den. Squirrels put twigs, **moss**, and leaves inside. High off the ground, they are safer from danger.

# Trees

Where do you like to hang out? Orangutans hang out in trees! They eat, sleep, and play in the treetops. Their long hands and feet can grip branches. Orangutans swing through the **rain forest**!

High on tree branches is where the sleepy sloth lives. It rests for most of the day. When it wakes up, it doesn't have to move. It finds fruits and leaves to eat on the branches.

A green tree python sleeps **coiled** on a branch. It is the same color as the leaves. This helps it hide. It hangs down to look for food, surprising **prey**.

Who can change its color? A
chameleon can! It lives mostly on
trees. That's where its favorite food is!
A chameleon catches **insects** with its
long, fast tongue. Yum!

Tree frogs are named for where they live—trees! Being green helps them blend in. Tree frogs don't like coming to the ground. They use their sticky toe pads to jump and climb through the trees.

*Knock! Knock!* Woodpeckers **peck** at trees. They peck to find food in tree bark. They also peck a hole to make a nest.

*Who's there? Baby woodpeckers!*

# Burrows

Skunks live in forests, deserts, and cities. They use their claws to dig **burrows** underground. In winter, 20 skunks may share one burrow! How many people live in your home?

*Buzz!* A cicada is an insect. It lays its eggs on twigs or branches. After they hatch, tiny cicadas fall to the ground. They dig burrows in the dirt. Cicadas live underground for 2 to 17 years!

A cicada coming out of the ground

A chipmunk digs a deep burrow in its forest home. Then it finds nuts and seeds on trees. The chipmunk uses its burrow like a cupboard. It stores food there for the winter.

When do you sleep? A badger
sleeps during the day! It uses its big
front claws to dig long tunnels to its
bedroom. At night badgers come out
to hunt.

Rabbit families are very big! Rabbits dig a big burrow underground. The burrow has many rooms and tunnels to keep the family safe. A rabbit burrow is called a **warren**.

A meerkat lives mostly in the African desert. It has a big burrow underground. The burrow has many ways to go in and out. A meerkat will pop up from its burrow in different places!

Have you heard of a **molehill**? It's where a mole lives! A mole digs a burrow. It makes a heap of dirt called a molehill. The burrow has rooms for eating, sleeping, and for babies!

# Shells

Can you take your home on the go? A turtle's shell is part of its body. It is also its home. A turtle can tuck inside its strong shell to stay safe.

An armadillo curled up in its shell

An armadillo looks like it is wearing hard shells all over its body. Its name means "little **armored** one" in Spanish.

When in danger, it does not fight. It runs away or curls up into a ball!

Some shells are more **delicate**.
Snails have a **spiral** shell that covers
their slimy bodies. The shell can chip at
the edges. But the snail is safe inside.

An oyster lives in the water. It has two shells. The shells can open or close like a mouth. Some oysters can make a pearl inside their shell!

Lobsters live in cold ocean waters. As a lobster grows, it loses its old shell. Then it grows a new one. The new shell is soft. But soon it is strong and will keep the lobster safe.

A hermit crab can choose its shell!
It finds an empty shell or other object
in the sand. This protects its soft body.
As the crab grows, it finds a bigger
shell to call home.

# Glossary

**armor** (AR-muhr)—bones, scales, and skin that some animals have on their bodies for protection

**burrow** (BURR-oh)—a hole or tunnel used as a home

**coiled** (COYLD)—lying or wound up in a circle shape

**delicate** (DELL-uh-kut)—easily broken

**insect** (IN-sekt)—a small animal with a hard outer shell, six legs, three body sections, and two antennae

**lodge** (LODJ)—the dry area inside a beaver's den

**molehill** (MOLE-hill)—a little mound or ridge of earth pushed up by a mole

**moss** (MAWSS)—a type of low-growing plant

**peck** (PEK)—to strike or pick up with a bird's beak

**predator** (PREH-duh-tur)—an animal that hunts other animals for food

**prey** (PRAY)—an animal hunted for food

**rain forest** (RAIN FOR-est)—a thick forest where rain falls almost every day

**spiral** (SPY-ruhl)—a pattern that winds around in a circle that gets bigger or smaller

**warren** (WAR-uhn)—a network of underground tunnels built by rabbits for safety and sleeping

# Read More

Aleo, Karen. *Living Things Need Shelter*. North Mankato, MN: Capstone, 2020.

Evans, Shira. *Animal Homes*. Washington, DC: National Geographic Kids, 2018.

Marsh, Laura. *Animal Armor*. Washington, DC: National Geographic Kids, 2018.

# Internet Sites

*National Geographic Kids: Habitats*
kids.nationalgeographic.com/nature/habitats

*PBS Learning Media: Habitat: Animal Homes*
tpt.pbslearningmedia.org/resource/nat15.sci.lisci.anihome/habitat-animal-homes/

*Time for Kids: Animal Homes*
timeforkids.com/k1/animal-homes/

# Index

# About the Author

Nadia Ali is a children's book author. She writes in various genres and is especially fond of animals. Inspired by her kitty, Cici, she contributes pet articles and features to magazines and websites. Nadia was born in London and currently resides in the Caribbean, where she happily swapped out London's gray skies for clear blue skies. She lives with her husband and has two married daughters.